D0932472

The Hole Truth! Underground Animal Life

Kangaroo Rat's Burrow

by Dee Phillips

Consultants:

Brian L. Cypher, PhD, and Ellen A. Cypher, PhD
California State University-Stanislaus, Endangered Species Recovery Program

Kimberly Brenneman, PhD
National Institute for Early Education Research, Rutgers University, New Brunswick, New Jersey

BEARPORT
PUBLISHING

New York, New York

Credits

Cover, © Mary Ann McDonald/Corbis; 2–3, © Wayne Lynch/All Canada Photos/Superstock; 4, © Anton Foltin/Shutterstock; 5, © Age Fotostock/Superstock; 6T, © Jason Patrick Ross/Shutterstock; 7, © Michael Durham/Minden Pictures/FLPA; 8, © George H. H. Huey/Animals Animals; 9, © Banana Republic Images/Shutterstock and © Wayne Lynch/All Canada Photos/Superstock; 10, © David Kuhn/Dwight Kuhn Photography; 11, © Joe McDonald/Corbis; 12, © Creative Commons Wikipedia; 13, © Mary McDonald/Nature Picture Library; 14, © Lightwave Photography/Animals Animals; 15, © mlorenz/Shutterstock, © fivespots/Shutterstock, © Stephen McSweeny/Shutterstock, and © Denis Pepin/Shutterstock; 16–17, © Rick & Nora Bowers/Alamy; 18, © Jack Goldfarb/Vibe Images/Alamy; 19, © Mark Chappell/Animals Animals; 20–21, © Rick & Nora Bowers/Alamy; 22, © Wayne Lynch/All Canada Photos/Superstock, © fivespots/Shutterstock, and © Rob McKay/Shutterstock; 23TL, © Age Fotostock/Superstock; 23TC, © Zack Frank/Shutterstock; 23TR, © Todd Klassy/Shutterstock; 23BL, © Mark Chappell/Animals Animals; 23BC, © Wayne Lynch/All Canada Photos/Superstock; 23BR, © Mary McDonald/Nature Picture Library.

Publisher: Kenn Goin
Editorial Director: Adam Siegel
Editor: Jessica Rudolph
Creative Director: Spencer Brinker
Design: Emma Randall
Photo Researcher: Ruby Tuesday Books Ltd

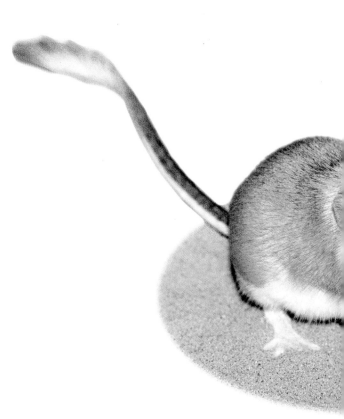

Library of Congress Cataloging-in-Publication Data

Phillips, Dee, 1967– author.
  Kangaroo rat's burrow / by Dee Phillips.
    pages cm. — (The hole truth!: underground animal life)
  Includes bibliographical references and index.
  ISBN-13: 978-1-62724-310-0 (library binding : alk. paper)
  ISBN-10: 1-62724-310-0 (library binding : alk. paper)
  1. Kangaroo rats—Behavior—Juvenile literature. 2. Kangaroo rats—Habitations—Juvenile literature. 3. Kangaroo rats—Life cycles—Juvenile literature. I. Title.
  QL737.R66P45 2015
  599.35'987156—dc23
                         2014019268

For more information, write to Bearport Publishing Company, Inc., 45 West 21st Street, Suite 3B, New York, New York 10010. Printed in the United States of America.

10 9 8 7 6 5 4 3 2 1

Contents

Meet a Kangaroo Rat

The sun is setting in a **desert**.

A furry face peeks out from a small hole in the ground.

It's a kangaroo rat.

The tiny animal hops out of its **burrow**.

It will spend the night searching for food.

sunset in a desert

All About Kangaroo Rats

Kangaroo rats belong to a group of animals that includes mice, rats, and hamsters.

There are 20 different types of kangaroo rats.

They all have plump bodies, long tails, and big eyes.

Kangaroo rats live in deserts and on **grasslands**.

grassland

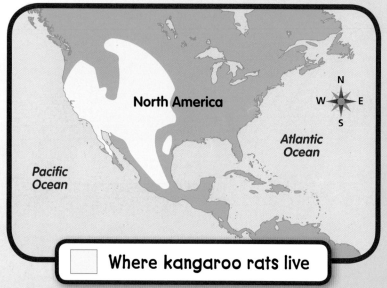

North America

Pacific Ocean

Atlantic Ocean

N
W E
S

Where kangaroo rats live

Kangaroo rats have big back feet. They move by hopping just like a kangaroo! This is how they got their name.

The kangaroo rat in this picture is life-size. How big is it? Measure its head and body with a ruler.
Use string to measure its tail.
Then measure the string with a ruler.

(The answer is on page 24.)

Building a Burrow

A kangaroo rat digs its burrow in sandy soil.

To make its home, the animal begins digging a hole with the strong claws on its front feet.

Then it digs lots of underground tunnels and small rooms.

A kangaroo rat uses one room for sleeping.

The other rooms are used to store food.

a kangaroo rat digging a burrow

A kangaroo rat's burrow may have up to 12 holes that the animal uses for going into and out of its home.

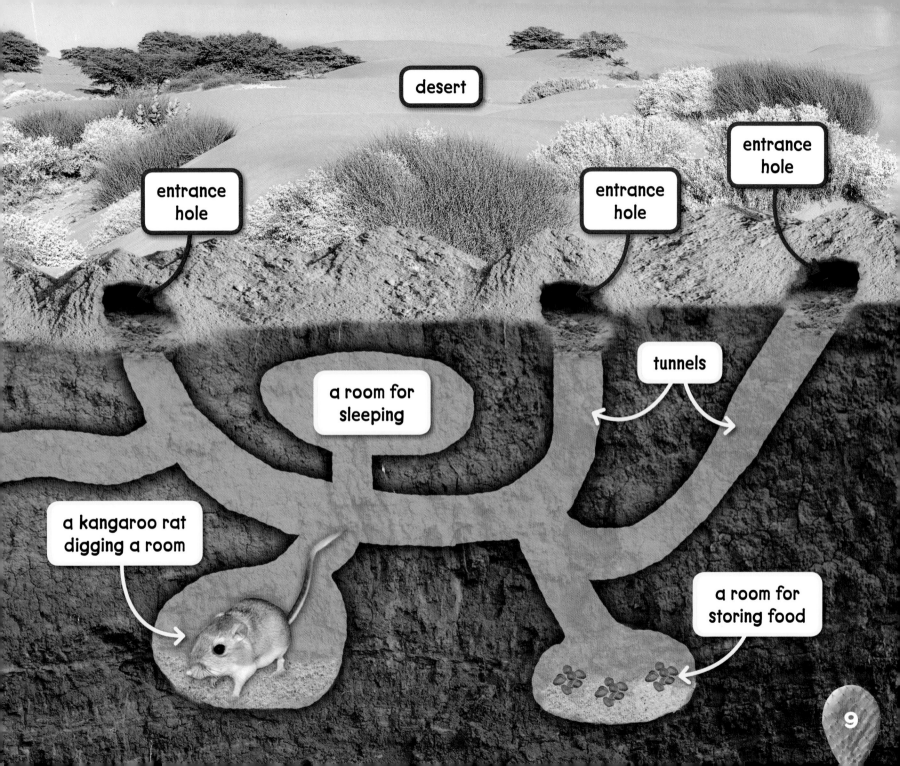

desert

entrance hole

entrance hole

entrance hole

tunnels

a room for sleeping

a kangaroo rat digging a room

a room for storing food

9

Night and Day

A kangaroo rat spends all day sleeping in its underground home.

When night falls, the animal leaves its burrow.

It spends the night searching for food.

When morning comes, the kangaroo rat settles down to sleep in its burrow.

a sleeping kangaroo rat

The areas where kangaroo rats live are often very hot in the daytime. Temperatures can reach more than 120°F (49°C) in summer. Spending the day underground helps the little animals stay cool.

a kangaroo rat leaving its burrow at night

What's on the Menu?

A kangaroo rat eats many kinds of seeds.

When it finds seeds, it picks them up with its front feet.

Then the animal stuffs them into pocket-like cheek **pouches**.

Once its pouches are full, the little creature goes back to its burrow.

It eats some seeds right away.

It stores the rest in one of its rooms to eat later.

Kangaroo rats eat seeds from plants such as mesquite trees.

mesquite seeds

Some types of kangaroo rats eat grasses, leaves, and insects, as well as seeds. Kangaroo rats don't drink water. All the water they need comes from their food.

a cheek pouch filled with seeds

13

Staying Safe from Enemies

When searching for food, a kangaroo rat must watch out for enemies.

Animals such as snakes, owls, coyotes, and bobcats all eat kangaroo rats.

To escape from an enemy, a kangaroo rat makes giant hops.

It can jump six feet (1.8 m) in a single hop!

The little animal quickly jumps away from danger to the safety of its burrow.

a kangaroo rat hopping

On nights when the moon is very bright, it's easy for enemies to spot kangaroo rats. On these nights, kangaroo rats spend only a short amount of time outside.

Kangaroo Rat Enemies

owl

bobcat

coyote

snake

Small snakes can slither into kangaroo rats' burrows. How do you think kangaroo rats stop this from happening while they sleep in the daytime?

(The answer is on page 24.)

A Burrow for Babies

Adult kangaroo rats usually live alone.

In spring, however, males and females meet up to **mate**.

About one month later, a female kangaroo rat is ready to have her babies.

She gives birth in her burrow.

The baby kangaroo rats cannot see, hear, or hop.

A mother kangaroo rat usually gives birth to between two and four babies at a time.

a mother kangaroo rat carrying her baby in her mouth

How is a baby kangaroo rat similar to and different from its mother?

one-day-old kangaroo rat

Little Kangaroo Rats

A mother kangaroo rat feeds her babies with milk from her body.

She spends the day sleeping with her babies underground.

At night, she leaves the babies alone for short periods of time to find food for herself.

By the time the babies are 14 days old, they can see, hear, and hop.

Now when their mother leaves to find food, the babies go with her.

a baby kangaroo rat

A newborn kangaroo rat weighs just a tiny bit more than a penny. An adult kangaroo rat weighs just a little less than a baseball.

These baby kangaroo rats are three weeks old. How have they changed from when they were first born?

The Babies Grow Up!

At five weeks old, young kangaroo rats are big enough to live on their own.

They know how to dig burrows.

They also know how to search for seeds to eat.

The young kangaroo rats leave their mother's burrow and begin their adult lives!

Kangaroo rats are ready to mate when they are about two months old. Female kangaroo rats can give birth to three or four **litters** of babies in a single year.

adult
kangaroo rat

Science Lab

Kangaroo Rat Escape!

A kangaroo rat is outside its burrow searching for seeds. Suddenly, it sees two enemies—a coyote and a snake! The kangaroo rat must escape by going underground.

Look at the picture and answer these questions.

1. Which burrow hole should the kangaroo rat hop to? Why did you choose this hole?

2. Which hole is farthest away?

3. Once the enemies have left, the kangaroo rat must leave its burrow again to find seeds from plants. Which hole do you think it should leave from? Why?

(The answers are on page 24.)

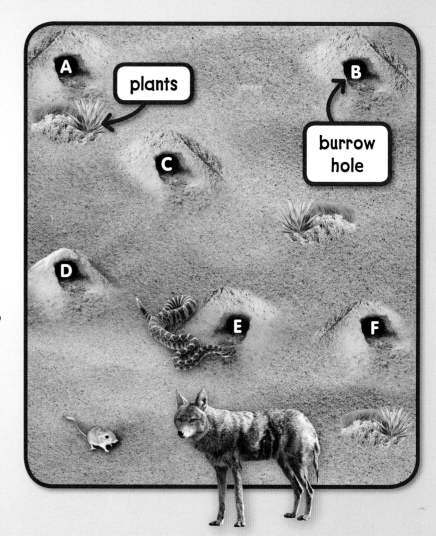

Science Words

burrow (BUR-oh)
a hole or tunnel dug by
an animal to live in

desert (DEZ-urt) dry land
with few plants and little
rainfall; some deserts are
covered with sand

grasslands (GRASS-landz)
dry places with lots of
grasses; only a few trees
and bushes grow there

litters (LIT-urz) groups
of animals that are born
to the same mother at the
same time

mate (MAYT) to come
together in order to
have young

pouches (POUCH-iz)
pocket-like parts in the
cheeks of some animals
used for carrying food

23

Index

Read More

Gardner, Jane P. *Fennec Foxes (Wild Canine Pups).* New York: Bearport (2014).

Lynette, Rachel. *Who Lives in a Hot, Dry Desert? (Exploring Habitats).* New York: PowerKids Press (2011).

Whitehouse, Patricia. *Rats (What's Awake?).* Chicago, IL: Heinemann-Raintree (2009).

Learn More Online

To learn more about kangaroo rats, visit www.bearportpublishing.com/TheHoleTruth!

About the Author

Dee Phillips lives near the ocean on the southwest coast of England. She develops and writes nonfiction and fiction books for children of all ages.

Answers

Page 7: From its nose to its bottom, the kangaroo rat is about 4 inches (10 cm) long. Its tail is about 5 inches (12.7 cm) long.

Page 15: From inside their burrows, kangaroo rats use their feet to push sand over entrance holes. This keeps enemies from getting inside.

Page 22:
1. Holes D and E are both close, but there is a snake outside hole E. So hole D is the safest choice.
2. Hole B is farthest from the kangaroo rat.
3. Hole A is the best one to leave from because it's closest to some food. The kangaroo rat can gather seeds and be close to safety.